Are you interested in a career in the entertainment industry, new to your position, or facing challenges leading effectively as a lady? You've come to the right guide! *For the Ladies: Becoming an Entertainment Leader* isn't just for Leading Industry Ladies, but for a community of women who are acclaimed bosses sharing similar challenges on their rise to the top.

Misogyny and societal norms have long influenced the imbalance of women in leadership roles. This book addresses the question: how do we prove the skeptics wrong? With time and change, women are now achieving heights our grandparents could never imagine, despite the distractions and challenges that come with rising to the top.

Author Tracyan Martin, an experienced leader in the entertainment industry, combines her chill, quiet, funny, yet assertive temperament to guide you through the intricacies of effective leadership. She emphasizes the importance of clear communication, balancing feminine and masculine energy, and staying true to your "why" — your driving passion for leading and effecting positive change.

This book includes personal anecdotes, such as Tracyan's journey from keyboardist to Music Director for GRAMMY Award-winning artist Melanie Fiona. Tracyan shares her experiences of overcoming imposter syndrome, building trusted relationships, and representing women of color in leadership roles.

Through her story and practical advice, you'll learn to navigate your leadership style, build healthy industry relationships, and maintain your dignity even when stepping down. Whether you're in music, show production, gaming, creative direction, sports, film, dance, or visual art, *For the Ladies: Becoming an Entertainment Leader* offers principles that apply across all fields.

Leading Industry Ladies, grab a pen and get ready to journal, reflect, and rise to the top!

TRACYAN MARTIN

FOR THE LADIES

BECOMING AN ENTERTAINMENT LEADER

Copyright © 2024 by Tracyan Martin

All rights reserved. This book or any portion thereof may not be reproduced or used in any manner whatsoever without the express written permission of the publisher except for the use of brief quotations in a book review.

Printed in the United States of America

Editor: M. Malcolm WritersTablet.org

Photographer Credits:
Cover photo: Jerry Metellus
Badge photo: Simone Acosta

First Printing, 2024

ISBN: 9798339104995
Writers' Tablet, LLC
Marietta, GA
United States of America
www.WritersTablet.org

*I dedicate this book to
the bravery of every
Leading Industry Lady
who dares to step out on faith,
walk in their God-given purpose,
and let their voice be heard.*

Table of Contents

Foreword 1
Preface 5
Acknowledgments 9
Introduction 11
Entertainment Relationships 15
Boundaries 23
Leading with a Heavy Heart 27
~~"Read the Room"~~ – The ROOM Is Reading YOU 39
Anticipate the Need 43
Delicate Delegation 53
Impactful Influences 61
The Entertainment Times 69
Appointed vs Assigned Leader 77
Feminine vs Masculine Energy 85
Becoming an Entertainment Leader 91
About the Author 95
My Notes 96

*"When you remind yourself of the why,
your passion will fuel and thank you."*

Foreword

Today is a glorious day, and I am honored to write the foreword for Tracyan Martin's book, *For the Ladies*. I'm Kim Burse, a seasoned music director with over two decades in the industry. Tracy refers to me as her mentor, and I am thrilled to know and work with her. She has much to share in this book, written for those who have a desire to work in an industry where men dominate. Her passion for empowering and encouraging women is commendable, and her journey is nothing short of remarkable – filled with the highest highs and the lowest lows. As you read this book, you will gain profound knowledge and insight into the experiences that have shaped Tracy into the ever-evolving talent she is.

Throughout my career, I have had the privilege of working alongside some of the best in the business, including Ricky Minor, Ray Chew, and Sheila E. My journey has led me to collaborate with music icons such as Beyoncé, Jennifer Lopez, Ciara, and Brandy, as well as contribute my expertise to major network television specials for ABC/Disney, Fox, BET, HBO, and, most recently, Country Music Television, where I proudly hold the title of Music Director. Notably, I was the Creative Music Director for the historic Grammy performance featuring Beyoncé and Tina Turner and composed the musical movie *Leave It on The Floor*. My role as Creative Music Director for BET's *Black Girls Rock* began in 2011, and I continued to bring my vision to the show for eight years. Disney also entrusted me with the musical direction of their annual Disney Holiday Special, airing on

FOR THE LADIES

ABC, for another eight years. Additionally, my work as Jennifer Lopez's Music Director spans more than a decade, including the Super Bowl and her sold-out "All I Have" Las Vegas residency.

In this compelling book, Tracy delves into the world of entertainment from a woman's perspective, sharing her journey to becoming a leader in the industry. This is a subject that Tracy knows intimately. From the very first time I met Tracy, her smile radiated ambition and drive, illuminating her path to success in the entertainment business. At that time, I didn't have a position for her, but her boundless energy and eagerness left an indelible mark on me. Tracy made sure to stay connected, always updating me on her projects and kindly reminding me that she was available if I needed anything. With fervor and determination, she expressed her desire to participate in one of the shows where I was Music Director, called *Black Girls Rock*.

In 2020, when the pandemic struck, I moved back home to Atlanta, GA, and serendipitously, Tracy was also there. As the pandemic persisted, offers to do show tapings in Atlanta (without an audience) began to roll in. This quickly opened up opportunities to work with Tracy. We collaborated on two shows for *Urban One Honors*, and her talent shone brightly. Then came the call to do my tenth show for *Black Girls Rock*, and this time, it was being taped in Atlanta. Now, it's not a question of whether I would call Tracy because I ABSOLUTELY would! Through her persistent communication and unwavering dedication, Tracy has become someone I trust – a leader, Music Director, and musician who masters her craft.

FOREWORD

In *For the Ladies*, Tracy not only shares her incredible journey but also provides expert advice and lifelong lessons for women aspiring to succeed in the music industry or any career. Her insights and experiences offer invaluable guidance and inspiration. This book is not just about empowering women and making them strong – women are already strong; it's about giving them the tools to shine and changing the way the world perceives that strength.

Kim Burse
CEO
311 Entertainment Group, Inc.

Preface

I'm Tracyan Martin: Atlanta native, professional touring/residential multi-instrumentalist, artist, and mentor. It's been quite the journey getting here. Growing up, I was an introverted kid and never had much to say; however, as I look back over my teenage years, I see very pivotal moments when I was being groomed to stand out and step up to the plate.

I was trombone section leader, gospel choir director, and head drum major in high school. I remember my dad had some combat boots, and I would take those too-big shoes and a curtain rod for a mace and march around the house pretending. It's safe to say I manifested being drum major and had faith in myself without context of what the task really required.

Have you ever wanted something so badly that it didn't even matter what it took? The idea of leading a 200+ piece marching band just resonated with me, as shy as I was. Now it did kick my butt both physically and mentally, but I committed to it.

Between Redan High School, playing piano at church, and being a part of my mom's performing arts school, these were truly impactful years when it came to me juggling multiple jobs and getting comfortable being out of my shell. I guess leading was in my cards as my parents, aka my pastors — PK here — and sister were also very instrumental as I watched them lead, manage, multi-task, and make things happen on a regular basis.

I've since gone on to perform in some incredible spaces and delve more into my leadership roles: from the 61st GRAMMY Awards, to touring with Fantasia and

FOR THE LADIES

Oprah, to serving as music director for Melanie Fiona, Janelle Monáe, and CeeLo Green, to project lead booking talent for Jammcard, to relocating to Las Vegas to join Cirque du Soleil, to teaching K-8th grade general music, to one-on-one coaching with aspiring musicians.

As a mentor, I also specialize in dispensing advice on leveraging your brand with endorsements and helping women navigate the industry as leaders while creating sustainable careers.

This journey has been beautiful, but it hasn't been without its failures, rock-bottom moments, and periods of stagnation. Life can be challenging in general, but as a woman with limited representation and guidance, it can feel especially daunting, lonely, and at times, almost unbearable. Perhaps this is something you can relate to and it explains why you're here. The path you're on will require guidance, and I'm here to help. As you take this journey to becoming an entertainment leader as a woman with me, my desire is for you to embrace your superpower, knowing that it can be done successfully because you're about to read how I did it. I look forward to imparting knowledge and enhancing your experience as a graceful and assertive leader.

Grab a pen and use the journal notes in the back of the book to plan your next steps.

.

(*Tracyan with numerous backstage badges)

Acknowledgments

First, I want to thank God for the courage to write this book, helping me maintain my faith throughout my career, and for protecting me along the way. To Dad, Mommy Bug, and Sissy Mel, who freely let me bang and beat on anything that made noise/music growing up as a little girl – I truly appreciate you for loving and supporting me on this wild journey. To my nephew Max, who is now taking on multiple musical gifts at six years old and thinks his auntie is cool, thank you for showing me how much you've been inspired. Without my nurturing family, I could not be where I am today.

Next, I can't thank my mentor Kim Burse enough for not only writing my foreword and guiding me through the years, but also continuing to pave the way for women in the entertainment industry who aspire to leave a legacy.

To my dear friends and extended family, thank you for the love you've given and being a shoulder to lean on throughout the obstacles I've endured. I'm grateful for every supporter who has believed in and cheered for me.

Thank you to my piano teachers, Mr. Fred and Mr. Eli, for imparting efficient fundamentals for me to be a better musician. Mr. Moore, a man of character and my Band Director at Redan High School, thank you for teaching me musically and instilling valuable life lessons. You saw there was more in me than just being a trombonist and seized the opportunity to have me lead as head drum major for the Blue Thunder Marching Band.

To Melanie Fiona, Janelle Monáe, and CeeLo Green, thank you for entrusting me to MD the band, and to Fantasia for allowing me to contribute to the creative process of the Sketchbook Tour. Also, I'd like to thank The Nevada Arts Council & National Endowment for the Arts for funding the publication of this book. Their unwavering support and investment in the arts community is an invaluable resource to which I'll forever be indebted.

Last but not least, I must thank Terri and the entire Writer's Tablet team for graciously and gracefully guiding me through this uncharted journey. Becoming a first-time author can be daunting, but Terri created the ideal environment for me to succeed. Her insight and experience as a leader are true gifts. She helped transform what was once just a few paragraphs in my phone notes into a tangible dream come true. For that, and for everything you've done to help me grow, I am truly grateful.

Introduction

So, you're here because you're interested in getting into a leadership role in the music industry, you're new to your position, or you've been in leadership but still find yourself having challenges leading effectively as a lady. Well, you've come to the right tour guide. *For the Ladies: Becoming an Entertainment Leader* isn't a book of gems only for Leading Industry Ladies, but for a community of women who are acclaimed bosses sharing similar challenges rising to the top.

From the beginning of time, it has been normal for men to hold leadership positions with a meager number of women doing the same. I personally think misogyny has played a factor in the imbalanced ratio of women to men in these roles. There are some people amongst us — both men and women — with a consensus that women can't handle being a leader in any industry capacity. So, the question is: how do we prove that group wrong? Sure, men are natural leaders, dating back to the biblical days. Regardless of the commonality of them being physically strong, it doesn't always imply they're stronger leaders. Society just has a way of influencing what we consider the norm.

Thanks to time and change, we live in an era now where women are doing a whole lot more among the higher-ups than our grandparents could've ever imagined. This is something great to celebrate as we've worked hard and we continue to make history. That easily translates as more ladies are leveling up their game and it's a beautiful thing to hear. Rising to the top comes with more drama than a juicy streaming series on Netflix, and there ain't nothing pretty about that part. Can I get an AMEN?!

Now, my temperament is chill, quiet, funny, but also assertive. We as women were born with an innate capacity to be patient and understanding. We are natural nurturers, and grace is just in our DNA. As easy as being graceful comes for me, this was not the same when it came to standing my ground. I had many challenges being assertive in the beginning of my career. I associated being assertive with being mean. I had no interest in creating drama or potential conflict, as I thought doing so would encourage such scenarios. Then one day, I heard these words that set me free: being assertive is simply being clear without aggression. So, it's not so much what you say, but how you say it. As a leader, say what you need to say, but do it with this in mind. The anxiety I initially experienced of not wanting to be misunderstood as a b*tch was greatly diminished with this gentle understanding.

If we took a poll and asked who has a master's in grace then asked right behind that, who has a master's in assertiveness, I believe one side will have more.... You picking up what I'm putting down? Your leadership style will be heavily impacted by your belief in yourself and your ability to always be clear, confident, and sure. That doesn't imply it'll be a breeze, but when times get rough, make sure you don't forget your "why".

Why do you want to be a leader? Your "why" is ultimately what drives your passion when things become overwhelming. Even with feelings of uncertainty, your love for leading and seeing positive change at the forefront will fuel your *assignment*. Regardless of what

INTRODUCTION

industry you're in — whether it's music, show production, gaming, creative direction, sports, film, dance, visual art, etc. — these principles apply throughout. What we know is that when a woman makes her mind up about what she wants to do, she gets it done by... you know the rest... BY ANY MEANS NECESSARY!! So, *Leading Industry Ladies*, let's dive in.

1. What part of leading resonates with you?
2. What area of leadership do you feel you need to work on?
3. Do you have a good balance of feminine vs. masculine energy?
4. How much experience do you have?
5. Are you willing to take risks?
6. Are you down to rock the boat with coworkers?
7. Are you able to bounce back after failing?
8. Do you have someone to look up to as a trusted mentor?

Entertainment Relationships
Relational Conversation Dynamics

One of the first things we will explore as a leader is your relationship with yourself and how you show up. Can you count on yourself to deliver in the game of life when no one else is watching? What's your track record?

Next, we will assess your relationship with a higher source, because you're going to need one. Guuurrrrrlll, ask me how I know! Highly recommended.

I grew up in church, so I depend on the Proverbs and principles by which I've learned to live to get me through day by day. Praying is also a part of that grounding that I consider important to me. Whatever way you find that works best to center your energy, go with that. That is a relationship in and of itself.

Afterwards, we can start addressing ways to build healthy relationships with others in the entertainment industry. I believe one of the best ways to get to know someone is through effective communication; where there's understanding. This is how you start cultivating solid relationships. Your ability to clearly communicate a task will play a major role in developing an efficient team.

Now, if the field you work in is a male-dominated environment, this may be where you're reminded that you're the 'Leading Industry Lady'. Maybe your first time will be or was a breeze, but it was daunting for me. Throughout this book, I'll share true touring stories with different topics to help paint the picture of the lessons I've learned and want to convey to you. It's story time!

Tour Tales with Tracyan
Melanie Fiona

The year was 2015. I remember waking up and getting ready for a trip to LA from Atlanta. It was my first day on the job. I'd just become music director (MD) for Grammy Award-winning artist, Melanie Fiona. This came about after having served as her keyboardist for five years and proving I could be loyal. Through the years, our communication with understanding and respect led to a circle of trust.

For those of you unfamiliar with the MD world, just know as an artist, your music director is your right-hand man/woman. They guide you creatively for hopes of delivering a successful show every time... NO PRESSURE AT ALL. I knew this meant I was going to have to work really hard, but my overall introduction to being a lady in leadership in the entertainment industry was BEYOND WILD AND EXCITING!

Shortly after celebrating, I did snap back into reality and, oh, BOY, was I in for an amusement park ride. There was work to do. My first official industry leadership experience was intimidating to say the least; a feeling you don't forget, but a monumental moment to remember. Once I got past imposter syndrome enough, I was able to think about just how powerful this statement — taking a stance on defying the odds and being a woman who leads a celebrity artist and their live show — really was. (By the way, I had to keep getting past imposter syndrome again, and again, and again.)

As Melanie's first woman music director, I represented a small entity as a Black woman leading. I was the only lady in the band, and for a good bit of time, I was the youngest in the crew. I was also reminded that I didn't have to do this alone. One thing I could depend on for my success with Melanie Fiona was the years I spent building a trusted relationship with her. There's a quote by Bobby Shields: "You can fix bad credit, but you can't fix credibility." Melanie Fiona knew I was credible. She knew I was loyal and capable enough to put a piece of her career in my hands. That same favor translated throughout the entire production crew as a benefit and led to historic moments that have become a part of my legacy.

The End

Right now, I want you to think about what statement you're making. For the people who haven't seen it done yet, you are the one to make them believe.

FOR THE LADIES

During my teenage years in Atlanta, I saw very few bands with women in them, much less woman music directors. It can be hard to imagine being something you didn't know could exist. Luckily, I'd finally seen who I was most inspired by as a woman boss in the music business – Kim Burse, A&R Rep (Artist & Repertoire Representative), Creative and Music Director Extraordinaire to the stars.

My initial introduction to this epitome of a 'Leading Industry Lady' was through a call to potentially play for Beyoncé, as she was her MD. I did not get the gig, but we were at least able to establish some familiarity. Thanks to social media, I was able to keep up with her whereabouts and accomplishments that continued to inspire me. It must have been seven to eight years before I was fortunate to meet her in person.

Have you met your hero, or do you wish you could? What qualities do you admire the most about them? Write those out so you can commit to checking them off as traits you aspire to attain and sustain.

What I've learned as a leader is that depending on your position in the company and that of the other person, your communication may be different. For example, as a music director, I may not speak to the artist like I speak to management. The method of communication may potentially be limited to email only, as opposed to a more personal text thread or Facetime. This can always evolve over time; however, communication rules should be handled case by case. Your level of communication will play a major role both individually and with the team. Your team wants to feel valued and appreciated. That said, you should learn to lead effectively through different channels, and be cognizant of how you should respond and how much or little you should say. This only comes with time and by understanding how your team best performs.

Maintaining Relationships & Leaving with Dignity

"Always leave in such a way that you can go back."

Another layer of relationships is dissolving one or having to step down. One thing we can attest to is this: if you've been with someone or a company for an extended period of time, no matter your rank, making a decision that your season is up can be difficult, even when it's obviously time to go. Whether it's romantic, business, or a planned short contract, your investment during that time was real. You're known to be loyal, but taking this step is a risk on many levels. You may concern yourself with other people's abandonment issues, their questioning if you're a person of integrity, and quite frankly their concern whether you can really be trusted moving forward. Those are all valid; however, in the case between you and life, you have to choose what's best for you.

In one of my highest positions as a music director, I noticed a certain season of my life was coming to an end. How did I identify it? My sleep, appetite, lifestyle, and mental health in general were declining, and I simply wasn't happy anymore. This inevitably started to affect my performance.

After several months of going back and forth with myself, I finally had the courage to do what was best for *me*. Now, I didn't just run away and relinquish my duties. I had questions about the best way to leave a situation as

FOR THE LADIES

a music director. My mentor, Kim Burse, really helped me with this one. I was sitting on her couch, and she simply asked, "What's your relationship with the artist and the manager? If you're really close with the artist, then it might be good to go directly to them and have a genuine talk."

That gave me so much peace and clarity on how to move forward. Regardless of what field you work in, these are questions to ask yourself if there isn't a protocol in place for resigning. Even if there is, always consider the relationships to make a better judgment regarding your method of departure. Here's where dignity comes into play.

First, what is dignity? It's the state or quality of being worthy of honor, self-respect, and grace. I ended up taking the email route with management and the artist, which was better in the moment. It allowed me to transition with logic at the forefront versus emotions because I had some of the latter connected with my reason for leaving. In my resignation letter, I did my best to bring awareness to how much I'd gained as a leader and how grateful I was for the opportunity, rather than what I thought was wrong. I did also mention — gracefully — that the workload was beyond overwhelming, and I needed to step down for health reasons. Of course, they took a hit as I played a major role being a director; however, I had decided *I* was most important in that moment. As you lead, please remember you and your relationship with yourself.

Another great leader in my life and someone I look up to is my high school band director. Mr. Moore has always been a man of character — a leader's leader — and would consistently use and live by these quotes:

"Lack of preparation on your part does not constitute an emergency on mine." As much as you desire your team to be prepared, you have to do the same.

"Excuses are tools of incompetence used to build bridges to nowhere and monuments of nothingness." This is an unjustifiable way to get out of things and says that you don't want to be held accountable. Therefore, it garners no results.

Along with these life lessons I learned in band, I've come up with an acronym for BAND that I refer to as B.A.N.D. Aids. These are words pertaining to you that will help with curating relationships, establishing a good reputation, and sustaining your career.

"B.A.N.D. Aids"

B - Building, Branding, Business acumen
A - Aesthetic, Ability, Attitude
N - Name, Networking, Negotiations
D - Discipline, Dependability, Dignity

Take these into consideration daily and keep them under your character and integrity umbrella.

Boundaries

As you continue this beautiful journey blossoming and becoming the leader you desire to be, consider your boundaries at every level. They define what you are comfortable with, the guidelines you set, and the limitations you place on a relationship that outline what you deem respectful.

One of the sure times your willpower can be tested is when you're at a party. One thing an entertainment company is going to have is a celebration, several. Sister Beyoncé said it best, "We like to party." If there are celebrities involved as in my case then things can get *litty*, real fast. You'll most likely have access to perks and benefits just by association with public figures. For example, you can get free clothes, shoes, gear, drinks, and a relationship worth flexing on social media when the hangs happen.

Speaking of get-togethers and parties, I've been to an array of them: rooftop, day parties, nightclub cameos, hotel parties, tour bus celebrations, dressing room

FOR THE LADIES

kickbacks, you name it. I could go on, but three fairly consistent things you'll find at these parties are alcohol, drugs, and temptations. One thing about liquor and drugs is they don't care what you do and will certainly release you from any inhibitions in the heat of the moment. That presents a bad problem because guess what: people gossip. Both men and women in this loose environment are more likely to let you know how they really feel in regard to physical attraction. This can be an audible expression or a pass on you. What makes matters worse is when someone comes to you, or you see them approaching someone else, knowing damn well they're not single. I've had both married and single men — tour managers, bandmates, production crew, and men from other camps — make inappropriate advances towards me.

There's a reference we say on tour, and that is "Don't be the 'tour hoe'." That name is not so much about what you do sexually, rather how many people you do it with. I can truthfully say I dodged that moniker, but only because of boundaries and discipline in that area and me wanting to consider my reputation. I've dated guys in the industry but I for sure wasn't tossing it all over the place at the same time; that's the difference. I have also fallen for a few men who stepped to me in instances where we weren't dating. To be honest, all of the passes and transactions weren't influenced by substances, but just sheer time and building relationships.

Think about when you're on tour: you're away from family, friends, significant others, and such, and your body has fleshly desires that you sometimes let get the best of you. Loneliness can be a detriment in and of itself. What do we do when we need to fill a void? We often medicate it and feed our minds with toxic behavior if we are not patient enough to explore positive outlets. These unhealthy habits can range from binging on bad foods, interacting with negative people, neglecting your wellbeing, or participating in potentially harmful recreational activities. Ultimately, we are in search of comfort by any means necessary when we don't have the fortitude to weigh out the discomfort or desires of our heart.

You may have lived your life on principles and morals, but those will go right out the back door if enough time goes by and there are assisting vices to help. It really comes down to an "F it" attitude… and don't let sh*t be rocky at home too. That's all you need to send you on a careless trip of decision-making. The one thing you have is your name, and you don't want to tarnish it by making an impulsive move 'cause you "feel a certain way". Your true success is predicated on how integral you are moving to the top. You can try to sleep your way up or work your tail off. I don't recommend the former as that lifestyle can backfire at any given moment. Has it worked for some people? I believe so, but to what extent? And what does that say about them as a person? How do you want people to view you on your come-up?

Another element of these business-ships is how you speak to men in front of family and how you address their significant others when in the same space. Some of these romantic partners might be cool. On the flip side, please believe some of their mates are coming out to the company parties with different agendas. They will side-eye you and think there's some funny business going on, not even gender-specific. That's their personal problem and not yours. I've literally had a male friend of 10+ years tell me we can no longer be friends because his wife didn't feel comfortable based on our history together, as

FOR THE LADIES

in, we previously dated. Mind you, that was 50-11 years prior to his marriage. I don't care how cool you are with a guy. If this happens, you have to go with it. Everybody won't be cool, so it's best to err on the side of keeping it *profesh*. Try your best to not show public favoritism. Don't text or call personal numbers unless it's an emergency and especially casually after hours. If at any point the dynamic of trusted friendship is established and well communicated, still proceed with caution. Use your intuition on how to best move forward without compromising your job security.

Keep in mind, no one immediately knows your boundaries, so it's best to verbally communicate them when you feel comfortable or if someone starts to walk that thin line. Also, if you exercise your limits towards others, it helps keep the line clear. I'm not saying it always works but it is a step towards ensuring you're treated the way you want to be handled. One of my great friends, Neal — guitar tech for Janelle Monáe — would always say, "You don't know boundaries until you cross them," and he wasn't lying. More importantly, when you make up in your mind what your boundaries are, keep them. At any point if you need to make adjustments to that list, be gracious with those around you who have to adhere to whatever that change looks like to you and be open about it. They may need time to adjust with you to better understand your why. Furthermore, be clear within yourself why these parameters exist for you. I avoided a lot of mishaps by simply maintaining my self-respect and keeping boundaries at the forefront of my life. For the ones that I didn't keep up, there were definitely unfavorable residuals to deal with. Save yourself some pain and agony. Keep reading, and you'll see.

Leading with a Heavy Heart

I believe one of the best ways to stay focused is to make decisions based on logic and not emotion; however, every now and then, things happen. I'd like to assume we've all experienced a loss, disappointment, failure, burnout, and lack of interest at some point as leaders. With that consideration, as whole women with hormones, we are not always privy to how we will respond to challenges and how our response will show up in our day-to-day tasks. There's a fine line between vulnerability and weakness when it comes to tough times.

Have you ever experienced something so embarrassingly traumatic that you didn't even want to share it with your closest friends for fear of judgment?

There's one instance in which you allow people into your personal space as a way to be transparent and informative. The goal is to give context that helps the team understand where you are and allows them to extend grace during your difficult time – *vulnerability*. The second instance is similar in that you inform your team of your hardships. The difference is, you make them your excuses and play victim. You seek sympathy in the hope of people understanding why you may need to temporarily relinquish your duties – *weakness*.

There've been quite a few occasions on which I was overwhelmed as music director 'in all thine ways', you hear. Talk about barely keeping it together! As soon as I would get to my car though, I would have a good ole circus cry. Yes, we are human, and there are people you should feel comfortable being around in whatever state of mind you're in, but realistically, those people aren't always around. Please understand: I'm not saying, "IT'S NOT OKAY TO CRY." Not at all! I do, however, believe there are better times to do so. Give yourself a pep talk to focus on completing the task for the team. If there's any reason you can't pull it together, you're human and it's understandable, so it's okay to give yourself grace; things happen.

I want to shift here and share a significant part of my story that led me to writing this chapter. This will be the first time for a lot of people to get a true look into my life and the battles I've overcome. Please prepare your hearts to be open while I take you on this journey spanning from 2009 to 2024.

Tour Tales with Tracyan
The Past, the Pain, and the Process

It was the night of March 30, 2024, and I was in the middle of my Cirque du Soleil show, waiting to play trombone on one of our ballads, "New York State of Mind". I was feeling emotionally fatigued that night from revisiting painful memories with my colleague while on break between shows. Out of nowhere, I felt this overwhelming sense of emotion. I was having flashbacks of the inception of my early hurts in the music industry. You really never forget them, even when you've conquered and surpassed those arduous places. So, we were right at the section in the song where we were to start playing, and my eyes just started filling with tears. Some were tears of sadness and the others were of gratitude and relief for getting through my past.

Let's rewind to 2010, when I was 22 years old. I was in ten-hour rehearsals with Musiq Soulchild preparing for upcoming spot dates. I'd just recently landed the gig with Melanie Fiona as her keyboardist. Sometimes you get these amazing calls to tour for months and then you never get a call again. One thing I said to myself when I started touring was, "I don't want to be a has-been in the music world." By attaining this new industry gig, I proved that I could remain relevant. When the invite-ONLY opportunity came up to audition for Mel, I initially declined the offer. My reasoning was, "I want to be loyal to Musiq. There's no way I have the heart to leave the artist who gave me my first real shot in the industry in 2009." I then decided it wouldn't hurt to at least get my feet wet. *Note to self: don't allow loyalty to override common sense.* Do artists 'feel a way' when you start spreading your wings? Absolutely! Should you let that dictate you taking chances on yourself? Absolutely not!

So back at the audition, Chuck Harmony, the MD, says, "I need for all the singers to raise their hands so we can get a headcount." The hands go up. He then looks dead at me and asks, "Why is your hand not raised?" I reply, "I'm not a singer. I play keys." Immediate awkward moment, but then we laughed, and it turned into an icebreaker. The assumption that I was there to sing goes to show you the uncommonness of women musicians in the industry. I was an anomaly, the only female keyboardist there of six.

So, the process moved along. It was a closed audition, but every invitee was in one room.

Chuck says to the musicians, "Whoever would like to go up first, just raise your hand." I know I have a millisecond to make a lasting impression, post-being mistaken for a singer, so I raise my hand first. I walk up there seemingly very brave but indeed very nervous. I do my audition alongside a drummer, bassist, guitarist, and singer. I feel like it was over in two minutes.

From there, I go stand back by the wall and watch everyone else as the auditions continue. The judges do their thank you's and Melanie's manager walks up to me at The End and says, "I think I might have something for you." Sure, I was like, "Okay, cool." I did not interpret that to mean I just got the gig but more like, "She works with other artists, so maybe she'll keep me in mind for future opportunities." So that was that and we said our goodbyes.

Several weeks went by and I remember receiving a phone call circa October 2010. Little did I know my life was about to change for the better. It turns out what the manager was considering me for was indeed Melanie Fiona's team. God knows I was glad I took that chance.

Now that you have context from the audition, a few weeks later, I'd find myself getting a real introduction into the music business. It became very real and unsettling.

My best friend on the Musiq hit pulled me to the side one day and said, "Sis, listen. I want you to know this and hear it from me first. The guys who were at the audition are saying you're not good enough to be on that gig. You're only on it for your looks, and it's just a matter of time before they realize you can't keep up, and you'll be off the gig before you know it." I was 'shook' and at a loss for words. I thanked him for keeping it real because he didn't have to.

It was in this moment that I experienced betrayal firsthand in the industry. What made matters worse was I knew these guys and thought they were my friends. It was silly of me to think such a thing. I was as green as they come.

My best friend and I went back into rehearsals, and I did my best to keep it together. At some point, I was at my keyboard station and tears just began to fill my eyes. I was so hurt, I was sad, and I was in disbelief. I was doubted, hated on, and disrespected. That became my introduction to the fact that you can't trust everyone in the industry space, much less in life. Hard Lesson Learned number one. You need thick skin in this business. I still had to pull it together, be present, and show up for Musiq, and I did like a big girl.

The next major distraction was sure to come along, and it didn't take forever to arrive. One thing I have to say is this: if you've been in entertainment long enough, working at a certain caliber, at some point you will get exposed to certain things you thought you'd never. The industry can easily exploit you and rip you to pieces if you're not careful. On that note, here is how my life ended up taking a turn down the wrong street.

FOR THE LADIES

In 2014, someone I trusted and loved dearly introduced me to cocaine. This lifestyle very quickly had a chokehold on me. The saying goes, "It is the appeal of the white girl." I never anticipated keeping it up, but that's not how drugs work. For the next five years, I would find myself battling a secret addiction. As a result, my life was beginning to spiral. I had no self-control. As a creative, I had a bad habit regarding lack of discipline in certain areas to begin with. That translated over into my financial life and health journey. Consequently, I started spending my bill money on this lifestyle.

Inevitably in 2017, I ended up losing my truck just two weeks after moving into my own apartment because I was irresponsible. I lied about my truck being stolen, ashamed of what had happened. Not only had I lost the first vehicle I had purchased on my own, but I'd lost my peace of mind, and lost myself. You would think that that would've made me stop, and I did briefly, but things got worse from there. An addiction will only get worse with time when life is *lifin'* and you can't catch a break.

I had been in a relationship all the while. He was also a musician and we had very similar upbringings. This seemed like a match made in Heaven, or so I thought. It would turn out to be one of the most manipulative adult relationships I'd ever been in. Things got rocky once I understood he wanted to be with multiple women and confronted him. I tried to give him grace over and over again. Some people just don't deserve your grace. Let me say it again for the people in the back: "Some people just don't deserve your grace." Don't allow your love for someone to dismiss your self-worth. Obviously his repeated offenses caused loads of stress, anxiety, and a broken heart. It's one thing to make a mistake in a relationship; however, it's another thing when it's a lifestyle. I was juggling a lot internally – feelings of inadequacy and blaming myself for not doing enough, all the while being a music director and band member for multiple groups.

Leading with a heavy heart became my survival mode. I had no healthy ways of coping with past and current hurts. The thing about addiction is, no one wakes up one day and decides they want to trash their life for no reason. It is simply self-medicating a symptom from a trauma bond over a period of time that takes you down. I was having anxiety attacks left and right, and my health and weight were plummeting.

By now, this was year five, which happened to be 2019. This was one of the best and worst years of my career, all in one. I had attained the most success in my career to date, but was also the saddest Tracyan I'd ever been. It wasn't until about a month before I started working with Fantasia that I was able to become sober and never look back again. It was only God who saved my heavy heart and me from this self-sabotaging lifestyle; I'm sure of that. "Weeping may endure for a night, but joy comes in the morning." (Psalm 30:5, AMPC) I found my joy again. He's always had a divine purpose for me to fulfill, so here I stand, restored as a faithful servant and leader.

The End

One of the biggest pills I've had to swallow is realizing that I could've not been here any longer. I know musicians personally who lived the same lifestyle but didn't live to see the next day. This exploitative industry can suck you

FOR THE LADIES

in so deep you feel you have no out. A lot of people in general are hurting silently, especially in the arts and entertainment world. Just know, it doesn't matter how far you go in the wrong direction, you can still turn around as long as you are breathing. I'm so glad I made the U-turn so that I can in return help the next person.

You may not have the same drug addiction, but you may have a habit that paralyzes you from being your best self. Maybe you prioritize someone else's needs so much that you've neglected yourself and your wellbeing. Maybe you're waiting on an apology from someone you once loved as an excuse to move on. Maybe you're prideful about your past and just don't feel adequate. No one knows you better than you. There are things that you've held inside that have never seen the light of day, even in what you deem the safest place. For years, I was embarrassed and ashamed of the lifestyle I adopted. I couldn't even think of what had happened without crying. Today, I stand tall and bold without pride, and I can share my story with power and authority.

I'm happy to say I never looked back after September 2019. Don't let a moment of your life or the people who judge you for what you did keep you stagnant. What you did/do is not who you are. As I once heard Oprah quote Maya Angelou at an end-of-tour cast party, "Your legacy isn't one thing; your legacy is every life you touch."

As women, we just want to feel safe and protected, but as Leading Industry Ladies, we stand on the frontline as soldiers. We are the safety and protection people look to. It will be important for you to be just as emotionally strong as you are physically, mentally, and spiritually! Sisterhood is something we all need and can thrive when we have that circle to pour into and pull from. When one is weak, the others will create a bond to make you stronger in your shortcomings. They will help you see every task through.

There are a few scriptures that have carried me through my downfalls. "To whom much is given, much is required." (Luke 12:48, paraphrased) "Don't be weary in well doing for in due season, you shall reap your harvest if you don't quit." (Gal. 6:9, paraphrased) "God's strength is made perfect in our weakness." (2 Cor. 12:9, paraphrased)

Adversity is a part of life, and I've always felt like it's magnified under the lens of leadership. It goes back to your relationship with yourself and how you decide to show up day after day. Accountability is a sign of maturity. I take responsibility for my decisions. I did what I did, and it was as real as it was painful. Find yourself a safe, healthy space or person to unpack your heavy heart. Mine became my best friend, Trunae, who never judged me along the way. She was there for the pain, the process, and the journey. With the help of therapy and the genuine love and support of Trunae, my family, and God, I overcame the most difficult times while leading as a lady.

Being relatable and understanding sometimes there are deeper issues we have to address has helped me with mentoring upcoming generations in this industry. Hitting rock-bottom in life can allow you to help someone else once you get up from it. These stories have now become a big part of my success story and help me be more effective in our community of ladies becoming leaders in the entertainment field.

"When life serves you lemons, make lemonade."

FOR THE LADIES

One of the things that will help you move forward on your journey is forgiving yourself for the things you never intended to take precedence in and over your life. One key to healing is to recognize and acknowledge what you haven't forgiven yourself for. What has happened in your life that is causing you to live under the shadow of shame and embarrassment? There are levels to healing just as there are layers to closure; it doesn't happen overnight. You may very well be reading this chapter with a heavy heart while managing overwhelming tasks. If you feel burdened in any way, chances are there may be more healing that needs to take place in your life and internal work to be done. Let this moment be an opportunity for you to start mending the broken pieces.

For the longest time, I would acknowledge what happened but not until writing about it did I find the courage to say, "I forgive myself" out loud. Here are a few statements to get you started that were real for me:

- o I forgive myself for not thinking I was good enough.
- o I forgive myself for neglecting my family and friends when I was battling addiction.
- o I forgive myself for letting people run over me.
- o I forgive myself for staying in that relationship when I knew I deserved better.
- o I forgive myself for not protecting my temple and my peace.
- o I forgive myself for making bad financial decisions I've had to pay for over the years.
- o I forgive myself for taking this long to acknowledge and forgive myself for the things that I've done out of character.

Take this time to think about what you haven't forgiven yourself for and be honest: write it down, take a deep breath and then I want you to audibly say, "I forgive myself for...."

Say this with me:

"I give myself permission to experience my own grace to its fullest potential."

Your life will and shall be enriched by doing this simple gesture. Grace comes with a lifetime warranty and unlimited benefits. It is the insurance policy for our lives.

Remember, the healthy relationships you build have the power to carry you even when you feel the weight of heavy burdens. The most important one that you'll have will always be the relationship with yourself. While leadership may feel like loneliness, the days of isolation are necessary. In those quiet moments, use that time to reset, readjust, replenish, refine, and even restart if you have to. May you continue to be courageous, tenacious, graceful, and assertive! I hope these words have fallen on your heart in ways that will propel you to be the best Leading Industry Lady you can be in the entertainment field.

~~"Read the Room"~~
The ROOM Is Reading YOU

Often, especially in creative spaces, the team will feed off your energy. In other words, you have a big impact and influence on the trajectory of your day solely based on your mood and how you show up. You are essentially controlling the room by managing multiple tasks and personalities simultaneously, while creating a space energetically conducive for the team to produce at a high level. My ATL side would just say, "If your vibe is off, chances are, theirs will be too!"

Never underestimate your presence in a room. This doesn't just go for familiar places. Even when you are new to an environment unrelated to work, your existence may make someone say, "I don't know who that is, but she seems like someone important." Have you ever gone out with your girls and a person walks in and just grabs your attention? Michael Jackson and Prince definitely had that effect on people. You didn't even have to see them to feel the shift. It's not so much in what you wear, but rather what you're carrying internally.

For many years I've used my hair as a part of my brand with signature colors. Sure, it brings attention to me, but what people are attracted to is beyond the look. It's simply a conversation piece to open the door to be able to serve. I use this as a conduit to connect with those to whom I am meant to be a blessing; however, even if you don't see me in person, my reputation precedes me.

As a leader, you shouldn't have to publicly announce your position. The way you carry yourself can literally inform people of your importance. My mom and dad look 20 years younger than they are, and people are always in awe to find out they're my parents. Now they do have great genes, but they also just have this air about them. Any time we go out to eat, someone walks up and says, "Y'all look like pastors." You would think they had on clergy garments daily. I'd be rich if I got five dollars for every time I heard this. It just goes to show you, the room really is reading you, even when you're not 'on duty', so to speak.

How can you have impact as a leader if your presence lacks power? It is a necessity to be able to control and manage the rooms you walk into. Ladies, those days you walk out in your sweats minding yo' business, looking like you looking, and guys are trying to holla… that's presence. Our natural, immediate side-eye shows up like, *He can't be talking 'bout me while I'm out here looking dusty.* Then we've had those days we get all cute and… blank stare; crickets.

There's nothing wrong with getting all done up. We love a good cute day, okaaaayyy? I will say this: please consider what you're feeling and be honest. Sometimes on a bad day, you have to dress how you want to feel, or how you want people to receive you, but be realistic with your expectations on that note. Some things you won't be able to mask from certain people based on how well you've established a relationship with them.

I always tell my mentees, "Every day you walk out your door, you're auditioning. You never know who's watching or watched you and it could be the fate to your success."

Tour Tales with Tracyan
Oprah

The year was 2019. I was in sound check with Fantasia for the Sketchbook Tour. I had a text message come in from an unknown number, so I ignored it in the moment. Later on, I went to Catering and decided to take a glance at the text. I read it, and immediately knew someone was playing games on my phone. The message read something like, "Hello, Tracyan, this is Eli and I work with DAYBREAKER. I was interested in chatting with you about going on tour with us opening up for Oprah."

Now you see why I thought someone was BS-ing. I brushed it off and went to go chill on the tour bus while I had some downtime. At this point, I remember it like it was yesterday. I revisited the text and asked was this for real, as I was still highly in disbelief. *'Cause ain't no way.*

So, the guy who said his name was Eli began to speak of a woman named Kiran who went by "Madame Gandhi". Now he had my attention.

FOR THE LADIES

About a year prior to this, I was in New York performing with Janelle Monáe at a festival. After we finished this show, this lady in all yellow came up to me backstage just oozing beautiful words. She said, "My name is Kiran and I swear I just couldn't stop watching you. Your energy was so electrifying." Keep in mind, I wasn't Janelle's music director yet, nor was I a frontline person. That was mainly Janelle and our six dancers. I was singing background vocals as well as playing keys, trombone, and guitar in the back. From my vantage point, I dismissed my ability to stand out because the band was the farthest from the audience, but boy, was I proved wrong! The day went on with me feeling special about what Kiran said, but I just kept it moving.

Back to the text, I later learned it was that one show that really moved her to refer me to Eli for this tour. She was a percussionist who was also joining the band for this run. I called my family frantically like, "You're not gonna believe this!!" Within one week, there were eight flights booked and confirmed for me to go out as a trombonist and keytarist opening with DAYBREAKER for Oprah's 2020 Vision Tour: Your Life in Focus. This was all because someone in the room was reading me – the right person at the right time.

The End

Anticipate the Need
"Script Not Always Included"

Any leadership role you walk into will usually have an outline of the job description. This outline may include daily tasks, goals, and the objectives for which you'll need to uphold certain standards to maintain the integrity of the company and its brand. A big part of the entertainment industry is branding and how the world gravitates towards it. The thing that is most unique about an entity, be it individually or collectively, is what people will associate with it the most. Understanding that will help you to begin to know what anticipatory moves you'll potentially need to make.

What does it really mean to anticipate the need?

My definition is being aware of the present circumstances, conditions, and environment while having the ability to think ahead and problem-solve.

FOR THE LADIES

Can you remember the last time someone anticipated your need? It offers you a sense of comfort like none other, and sparks a great deal of appreciation for them. It also makes you more likely to feel like you can depend on that person because they have paid attention to detail.

First things first: it's not magic, it's intuition, which I do consider to be very magical. Whether you believe in a higher power or not, one thing most of us can agree on is your intuition is a gift. When you can tap into your discernment, your sense of judgment is better for decision-making. There's no manual that comes with this, but we have to go heavy on the gut feeling. If you have a thought or idea, don't shut yourself down out of fear of it sounding ridiculous. It could be a game changer and enhance your experience as well as that of everyone on the floor.

Now, some days we will naturally be more or less in-tune, based on the conditions, environment, and circumstances surrounding our day. 'Conditions' are the circumstances affecting the way in which people live or work, especially with regard to their safety or wellbeing. The 'environment' is similar to conditions, but more related to the natural world as a whole or in a particular geographical area, especially as affected by human activity. Lastly, a 'circumstance' is a fact or event that makes a situation the way it is. So, what do you do on those 'OFF' days? You rely on what you know. Logic is a very powerful tool in a leadership position. It's okay to not know. I've never met a leader who knew everything. Remember, *you don't have to know it all.* I often say "logic over emotion" when trying to accomplish something as a leader. Of course, there are some exceptions, but this is a great place to start.

ANTICIPATE THE NEED

Regarding anticipating the need, the overall goal is to be able to come up with great ideas and quick solutions before a request. Also, you should understand how much of the team you'd need to rely on to complete the task. I grew up in church, where there is a big emphasis placed on your spirit. What is it telling you? My fellow bandmate at church is a very wise man. One night, he brought this quote to our attention in rehearsal: "There are three forms of sight – hindsight, foresight, and insight. Once you understand the purpose of all three, then you'll know what to do NOW." It just resonated with me so much when he said it. A big part of leadership requires you to use all of them. Your ability to anticipate the need is a culmination of each of these, and if you want to go far, you'll allow all of your sights to assist along every journey.

Hindsight: the understanding of a situation or event only after it has happened or developed.

Foresight: the ability to predict or the action of predicting what will happen or be needed in the future.

Insight: the capacity to gain an accurate and deep intuitive understanding of a person or thing.

I grew up in musical theater (Thanks, Mommy Bug!). Beyond the creative, here is where I learned the importance of a script and show cues for each act and scene. The director sets out the vision and devises a plan to create a successful show, top to bottom. This is no different from whatever your niche market is.

Essentially, as a leader, you are signing up to do something that you may or may not know how to do… yet. Let me take a side street and yell this for the people in the

FOR THE LADIES

back, front, and outside: "YOU ARE ENOUGH! YOU ARE ENOUGH!" Now you make it personal: "I AM ENOUGH!" Being enough doesn't imply you have all the answers or resources upfront, so release yourself from that pressure. If you were chosen for the position, then it confirms that affirmation: *You Are Enough.*

Remember, you have a whole team to rely on based on the relationships you have built with them.

"No great leader wins alone."

Now, that said, we all love a great plan and organization; however, that method can still fail. For all you amazing planners and anticipatory thinkers, what happens next? Just because you don't work in a creative space, that doesn't mean there won't be a need to be creative and innovative. Let me say it again, and be sure to read it slowly: Just because you don't work in a creative space, that doesn't mean there won't be a need to be creative and innovative. Everything can't be by the book. You are going to run into some surprise snags and have complaints that are valid. I like to reference this piece of advice often: "Never present a problem without a solution." Some things you may not be able to realistically figure out, but make sure you exhaust every possible option. Leaders have to consistently strategize and enhance systems that are catered to and curated specifically to suit the business. When there is no script, you have to tap into your creativity and anticipate the need. Think outside the box.

Tour Tales with Tracyan
Janelle Monáe

So, the story begins on the Sprinter, our standard ground transportation for crew, band, and production team as we're headed to rehearsal. Generally, there's a plan of action for the day set in place; however, artists have free will to make changes at any point the desire hits them. Well, this was one of those days. I received a call from Janelle Monáe, and she basically wanted to change up the show. As one can imagine, performing the same set back-to-back can become a bit mundane. As creatives, routines sometimes plague us, so with every understanding, I know she absolutely had every right to make a last-minute call. Now, that said, I very gracefully and slowly announced, "Heeeyyy, guys. Soooooooo, Janelle would like us to switch up some things musically, play with some different arrangements. I don't know what exactly this will evolve into, but we are going to try some things. This is also a collective adventure. If you feel something could go and work well without messing with the integrity of the overall show, let's give it a shot."

Delegation always wins.

Meanwhile, my mind was quite overwhelmed creatively as I was trying to at least start fleshing ideas out to create the direction of the day. Remember again, the leader sets the tone. I didn't know where it would end up, but I was aware that if I had a start, everything would follow. So, we proceeded to start making changes. I may have sent Jane (that's Janelle's nickname) a few updates so she would know what to expect to be different rather than coming in completely surprised. The arrangements were evolving into something cool… so I thought. We started locking in and finding the rhythm of the day.

One thing to note as a leader in the industry is this: never get married to an idea until the boss gives it a final go. It's like catching fish, but not being able to fry them just yet. Keep them alive but also understand you may have to throw them back in the river. We kept fishing, throwing in new bait for different fish, and we were catching some. It took time for sure even after getting into the groove. Figuratively speaking, the weather was right. The water was shallow enough to see there were fish all around and the time was right. I don't fish in real life, and quite frankly I'm terrified of fish flailing all over me. (If you know, you know.) What I do know is you don't have to be a fisherman to know there's a good time, *a better time* to fish. Timing is vital in this industry.

So finally, Jane arrives. I don't know what I was feeling in the moment, but as I'm writing I can think of a few things that were going through my head. *Is she going to hate it? Will she love it? Will it inspire something in her? What just happened altogether?* I was nervous in the moment about it all, because it was a first. We greeted and I spoke to her about the changes that were made and one by one, we went through each act. There were a total of four, and she listened with her ears, eyes, and heart. Jane ended the day by saying, "It's cool but I want to change it back."

One thing's for sure, it's easier to go back from this vantage point; however, as a leader, I understood that she was in search of something that we had not achieved just yet. Keep in mind, we were preparing for a big outside show in the harbor in New York. There was still pressure after our nine-hour rehearsal to present something that would ignite a spark in Janelle.

Out of nowhere, I had a thought, and it couldn't have been anything but God. I walked over to Jane and our creative director Jemel. I sat on the floor humbly, as I was getting ready to say something that would either help change the direction of the evening or get vetoed. I prefaced it like this, "Go with me for a second." This is the buffer I use when I'm not sure of what I'm about to say… how it'll be translated and/or received. I looked at Jane and asked, "Have you ever DJ'd?" She replied, "Yes," but kind of on the timid side. I then asked, "Have you ever DJ'd in your show?" She gave a sure "No." Still sitting on the ground, I took a deep breath and put my head down then looked up at her and said, "I think you should DJ in your show." Immediately, her eyes got big, but with a light that I hadn't seen in a while. It was at that point I realized I had figured it out. I'd found something that would reignite her love for performing her own shows. She's truly a performer's performer. She was instantaneously inspired, and however daunting the task was, she was up for it.

Fast-forward, we did the show, and it was her debut performance DJ'ing live in her set. We made history that day!

The End

Now, you may ask yourself what that story has to do with anticipating the need when Jane was the first to request changes to the show. Well, in real time, my idea was the immediate solution per her request; however, there is duality in this. It wasn't until the 2020 pandemic that I realized it was actually an anticipatory action simply because it gave her something to feel alive for when all the live shows were put on halt. We had over 28 tour dates on the calendar that were abruptly wiped away from us. The one thing that she could do safely, virtually, as an artist that was innovative and fresh to her brand was DJ. No one could've guessed Covid was coming our way. It certainly took its time and many things from us. So, I provided a means of survival a year prior to the first need that she could hold onto for her creative spirit in a time of despair.

Artists are sensitive to their craft and if their livelihood is snatched away, it's a huge loss in the heart space. This is what makes you feel alive, like you have purpose. I'm speaking from personal experience as I lost over 40 shows that year with no back-up plan. I felt displaced and, quite frankly, irrelevant. All I knew regarding work was performing. I had to walk away from music and get a job as a caregiver caring for the elderly with cognitive impairments and stages of dementia that were heartbreaking. Those moments sure brought a different perspective to my life when it comes to gratitude. Losing your independence is an eye-opener but it goes back to making the most of your life while you have the autonomy to do so. If there was something that gave you and others hope in such tumultuous times, you would feel good about it, right? This is what DJ'ing did for Janelle. Years later, her DJ persona has evolved, and is gaining acclaim as she is being booked all over as DJ Johnny Jane.

Don't be afraid to challenge the people who are over you. Have faith in yourself knowing you're there for a reason. I could've left it alone, but I understood my destiny was connected to the success of hers. What you don't do, versus what may come to mind, could very well keep someone from blossoming into their higher, best selves.

If you have to do it scared, do it. If you have to do it unsure, do it. If you have to do it knowing it may jeopardize your position moving forward, do it. Trust your gut, and the rest will follow.

I couldn't be more elated about the success and acclaimed notoriety Janelle has gained as a DJ by putting herself out there. Most importantly, because of my courage, that has now become a part of my legacy. I answered a request, anticipated an unforeseeable need, and understood the assignment.

Delicate Delegation

Giving direction gracefully and assertively while delegating tastefully is a true art form.

So again, the tale is women in leadership can be b*tches sometimes. Now, some people can agree there are some bossy bosses – women and men; however, let's debunk the myth that a woman giving direction is automatically associated with such a disrespectful stigma. Remember, we discussed being clear without aggression, so we got that out of the way. There are two major things to consider when preparing to divvy up your workload; delivery and understanding are key. Timing is also important; however, sometimes you may not have the autonomy to wait for what you deem a 'good time'. Once you've anticipated the need, it's time to figure out what you need from each team member or group. It is always best to write it down first. You should at least make time for that. The more organized you can be upfront, the less you have to repair and correct on the back end.

FOR THE LADIES

I spent a lot of years saying, "It's okay. I got it. No thanks, I don't need any extra help." For the love of God, I was drowning in puddles and driving myself into the ground. What is self-inflicted stress for $1,000, Alex? My pride didn't want to have people doing 'extra' things at my expense. People actually do like to feel needed and sometimes, it's their job. Yes, you can be a hard worker, but let's embrace teamwork as the real power move. Learn to say what you really need to say. Be encouraging, ambitious, and grateful for your team. Appreciation goes a long way when you need assistance.

The other beautiful thing about delegation is, it sets you up to become a predecessor to your successor. One of the clear signs that you've done a thorough job leading is when things go smoothly in your absence. Leaders often get burnt out because they're the only ones who can do their job. Always consider your back-up plan and who you'll have to stand in your place when you are unable to be present or deciding to step down and transition, be it temporarily or permanently.

As a woman, there are very specific variables that could place you in the position to have to step away. You may have to take a maternity leave; perhaps you're a single mother with no help from the father and need to tend to your child, or focus on women's health matters. It is so important to take time to rest and rejuvenate. The benefits of preservation are indeed long-term. When they say health is wealth, it truly is. What good is a successful, dazzling career in entertainment if your failing health is at the mercy of what you put your vessel through? What is your diet? What is your exercise regimen? We have to constantly consider our health and how we show up each day to be our best. I'm definitely guilty of working to the

DELICATE DELEGATION

point where my body has no choice but to shut down – not a great place to be. Have you been there before? On the record: please go see a doctor if something feels off, ladies. We don't like to hear potential bad news, but better safe than sorry before it's too late. There is a fine line between working hard, pressing through, and having an unhealthy work ethic. So again, I say to you, please use delegation as a tool to help take the load off you.

Let's look at three different leading styles and how exercising delegation will work best for you.

The Bossy Leader – Everyone knows she's the boss, and they hate it. She power trips because she's slightly insecure and feels disrespected. She feels the need to over-prove herself and micromanage.

The Pleasing Leader – She says yes to more than she can handle, doesn't take risks, is afraid of disappointment, is afraid to say "No", has challenges with delegating, and simply gets burnt out.

The Leader's Leader – She does business assertively with grace, is consistent, is courageous, takes accountability when at fault, and has a strong concept of her team in regards to how they best receive and understand task requests. She can be trusted.

(Which one are you, truthfully?)

So, I'll tell you this: I've lived two of these phases: Pleasing Leader and Leader's Leader.... In retrospect, I identified three areas that put me in the Pleasing Leader category: I rarely delegated, didn't challenge my team, and was a yes woman. I had to grab hold of each area and take control of my destiny. I would've never become a Leader's Leader with any of these attributes.

Let me ask you a question: do you know what you sound like? Yes, you've heard your voice all your life. It seems like a silly question, but I would encourage you to record yourself and listen to how you sound sometimes. Whether you're delivering information or just in a casual conversation, it's good to hear yourself from a different perspective. Do you sound inviting? Do you sound timid? How is your diction? Do you sound assertive? Do you sound annoying? I'm from the South, so I sound country from time to time. The southern drawl is real. ATL people have their own situation. #IYKYK

Use Your Words Wisely

Let me ask you this: have you ever had a close coworker get promoted within the company? Have you ever been promoted to a leadership position before someone who started working at the same time or before you? I've been in both scenarios. That second one, *whew, chyle!* There are so many avenues to consider when you're moving up the ladder, but more importantly when you're at base level.

Let's rewind to your first day on the new job as a regular employee. Perhaps you were planning to just be a background person and do what was expected to make some money. Maybe your end goal was to become a general manager or supervisor. Either way, we all have a first day, and it's a taxing process getting familiar with new areas, systems, and a whole new group of people. Some of them will eventually become your friends. Some of

DELICATE DELEGATION

them, God bless 'em; moving on. Those blossoming relationships will only be as much as you allow them to be. I'd like to think working in creative spaces makes it easier to connect and vibe with people organically, versus the straight-up corporate world. Use that to your advantage. Feeling comfortable with colleagues over time is a natural progression. Some of us will eventually share secrets, family business, and personal opinions in the workspace. This can and may be a harmless thing but beware if you get that promotion offer. The things you and your homegirl or homeboy gossiped about could come back up and turn on you. How you start is essential to you moving up in a company.

For the most part, I'd never had any outrageous drama with anyone in the music industry whom I consistently worked with. ATL moment: "Ween had no beef." It wasn't until things started shifting regarding my position that things started to change. This is a delicate, fragile, and very uncomfortable and uncompromising position to be in. Again, regardless of the industry/business you work in, it can be extremely awkward becoming your coworker's boss. This can easily be someone who started out as a stranger then became your friend, or someone you may even have grown up with. Maybe you have brunch on the weekends, and although you're completely unrelated by blood, their kids call you Auntie by default. It's good to consider that the shift in your position may be a difficult thing for your coworker to process, while you're celebrating great news. Some of them could be dealing with egos and pride, and some may just feel sad they didn't get the promotion. That's not anything you need to concern yourself with. Don't let it get you off your A-game. STAY FOCUSED.

FOR THE LADIES

I once had a friend who vetted me for a gig in 2018 and eight months later, I became the music director. As happy as I was, I felt a little bad because she was a big reason why I was even on the hit, and she had wanted the position, unbeknownst to me. This was someone I considered to be like my big sister. She was also very instrumental in me getting my first industry gig in 2009. You see, there were layers to this. Here was where there was no script for me to lean on, so I used my loyalty/common sense, if I can say it like that. I decided to call her personally before the official big news was released to the public. I was nervous walking into the conversation, but I was clear with my intention. What I wanted the most was to show my appreciation and that I truly valued our friendship. We'd been friends for nine years prior and have remained friends. As much as I didn't want our dynamic to change, it was inevitable. It just got weird at some point and truthfully, I didn't know how to make it better or if I could fix it at all. I still had to delegate tasks, understanding she wasn't really vibin' with me like that. We eventually had a heart-to-heart, and the wheels started turning again after what seemed like a lifetime; I'd gotten my friend back. It doesn't always end that way, so be realistic with your expectations from familiar people. Navigating business-ships with friends is a true art form if both parties can successfully manage when to turn it on and off. Respect has to always be at the forefront. Logic over emotion; it'll protect you.

Another difficult dynamic regarding delegation is learning to deal with people who don't respect you in your role. It just comes with the territory. I don't care how pleasant, likeable, and easy to work with you are, you can't convince somebody to like you who… ughhhhh… just doesn't like you!

DELICATE DELEGATION

One of my biggest pet peeves is feeling disrespected. It's a violation to your belief system in yourself and the value you bring to the table. What I can tell you now is that that passive 'ish' *ain't gone work* here in this scenario. This is when you might need to engage your supernatural mode of grace with assertiveness. You can expect Resting B Face from them, a lackluster greeting, disregarding your emails, shenanigans as petty as they come, and just downright *blah* energy. If it becomes unbearable to work together, you can always go to the higher-ups if you have access to them. You want to maintain your composure at all costs. There's no need to meet them with that energy, although every now and then, we'd all love to let somebody have it one good time. You may have just had someone immediately pop into your head. KEEP CALM, SIS! "Woosah." These kinds of people may feel like the resident bully. Pick your battles wisely. Don't let that get in the way of the assignment.

No time for fear! I have a saying, "I don't do nervous energy. It's the difference between me trying to get sh*t done while you're trying to get comfortable." Leadership is not a Comfort Zone Inn. You have to keep showing up to accomplish tedious tasks and be as consistent with that difficult person as you would with someone who's cool.

"Effectively communicate directives and delegate when needed."

Impactful Influences

I'm going to take two different angles here regarding influence. One will be an emphasis on your influences and the second will be how you influence others. The daily decisions you make for your life and habits you've developed can and will show up in the way you lead. These are areas in which you may potentially be forced to grow over a short period of time, GUARANTEED. There are a lot of factors as to who you are, why you do what you do, and the qualities you possess.

Let's talk about the H word: habits. There are some people who grow up and say, "This is just the way that I am." Maybe that person is a big procrastinator, an over-thinker, someone who doesn't place a lot of importance on their health, or someone who lacks accountability and discipline. The biggest challenge for me was discipline. As a true creative, structure was just not one of my strong points. I lacked organizational management, and my ability to plan ahead in certain areas was subpar. Creative

FOR THE LADIES

people in the arts love to let life live and be. We don't subscribe to routine often, if I can speak for a few others and myself.

Depending on your specific discipline, naturally adapting and adopting new habits/lifestyles is sure to be a factor. If you get a job at a fast-food burger chain, chances are you're going to start eating more burgers. What if you get a job working at an electronics store? You're more likely to start making more tech purchases. If you work at a gym, you might be more inclined to choose a healthier lifestyle. The influence of your environment and the conditions and circumstances surrounding it play a major part in who you are and what you do.

Another thing to consider is your family. Even if it hasn't directly been said to us, we've all at some point heard the phrase, "You're just like your mom." "You're just like your dad." We've come right back to the statement, "It's just the way that I am." If you're fortunate to still have your parents, it's a beautiful thing to start asking them questions about their upbringing. We often become our parents without even knowing it. This can be good or bad, depending on how you apply it to your everyday life. That being said, when you consider generational curses, you're going to want to be aware and careful that you break that mold. You'll only know, though, if you take the time to really communicate and learn about your family history.

Another big influence that impacts the way you are is religion. I read in *Collins Dictionary* a simple definition of religion: "belief in a god or gods and the activities that are connected with this belief." For Christians and Muslims, some of those activities may include the rituals of praying, worshipping, and attending church/mosque. If you really look deeper into it, these are early lessons for teaching discipline. Here is where you find yourself getting into a routine and developing systems and practices by which you abide.

One of the biggest benefits I found regarding my religion was the sense of grounding it brought to my life. When I moved out to Las Vegas, it wasn't until I started attending church ten months post-relocation that I started to feel grounded again. As a Pastor's Kid, aka PK, I spent several days at church throughout the week. It came with the territory. If you know, you know. However, it played a major role in how I see, treat, serve, and consider people, as well as my tendency to give them grace and forgiveness.

Another part of life that was pivotal about attending church was seeing and understanding the role of a leader. My parents were both pastors and shepherds of their sheep. I had a front-row seat as they sacrificed their time, house, family, money, wisdom, resources, and listening ear. Some people were appreciative of their good works and others took advantage, but I never saw them publicly act out of anger and character when they were mistreated. One of the big things to know about leadership is that being the head doesn't always determine the respect you will be given. It's up to you to be mature and not react with the same level of disregard and disrespect.

So again, my first and biggest influencers as leaders were my parents. The lifestyle you live will be influenced by your surroundings and upbringing. Always be mindful of the impact they will have on your discipline, health, vices, and habits. Some things you will have to unlearn and rewire to become the dynamic leader you aspire to be.

FOR THE LADIES

The other way I want to look at influence is the impact you have on the people you encounter. Thanks to technology, we can reach a whole lot more people than when there was no Internet. Social media is a powerful platform and a viable tool for reaching the masses. If you revisit your answer to the indirect question I asked in the first chapter, "What statement are you making right now?" that is your influencer tool.

For the longest time, I can remember saying, "When I grow up, I want to be a veterinarian or work in the medical field in some capacity." My mom has worked as a Registered Nurse longer than I've been alive. She influenced my desire to go in that direction. Not once in my childhood did I wake up saying, "I want to be a music director in the entertainment industry," because I literally didn't know I could even have a chance at it. It's hard to imagine wanting to be something you didn't know could exist.

Let's take Venus and Serena Williams as prime examples. You don't have to play tennis to know exactly who these women are. I had never even played tennis prior to relocating to Las Vegas. It just wasn't common in Atlanta to see tennis courts or players during my youth, much less black ones. One thing I was going to do was play street ball on the court or in the residence cul-de-sac. Things have since changed in "The A" as parks have evolved beyond the basketball courts. As for Vegas, there are tennis courts everywhere out here. Thanks to my new city and Mad Apple bandmate, JF, an avid tennis player and coach, I was encouraged to explore the sport. As they say, "Monkey see, monkey do."

IMPACTFUL INFLUENCES

Back on the note of how your environment plays a major role in the things you do, perhaps I was also curious because my mom mentioned she played, but I hadn't seen it with my own eyes. Nonetheless, it turns out I love tennis and feel like I can relate to the Williams sisters in a way. Now, I have no plans on trying to become a pro; however, there are many people whose careers have indeed been positively influenced by theirs.

Here you have two black sisters who grew up in a middle-class family in Compton, California. Their father, Richard Williams, didn't have the money to put them in tennis lessons, so he bought an instructional book and taught them what he could. During the Open Era of professional tennis, beginning in 1968, there was little to no representation of young black women in tennis. The sisters managed to make history and inevitably became trailblazers. With Venus winning seven Grand Slams and Serena 23, the bar has been set and established for any little black girl to believe they can do the same. It's evident that their accomplishments had an impact on the world, as they are still relevant in pop culture in 2024 when it comes to sports entertainment.

I'd like to specifically highlight one athlete who benefited from their hard work and the path they paved. Hailing from Atlanta, Georgia, Coco Gauff was inspired to play tennis at the tender age of six after witnessing Serena win at the 2009 Australian Open. She stuck with it and grew up to become a pro tennis player, facing and beating Venus, one of her idols, at Wimbledon when she was only 15. Coco went on to win the U.S. Open Women's title in 2023. She now gets to inspire little girls who look like her as she continues to raise the bar for young athletes and pursue greatness in her own career. That certainly speaks volumes to the impact of influence and what it can do. Don't ever think kids are too young to know what they want to be when they grow up.

Ironically, Coco's father initially wanted her to become a basketball player. This isn't surprising considering we're from the same city and during my childhood in the late 80s and 90s, it wasn't out of the norm to push basketball as an attainable career for women in sports. Even down to my middle school years, myself and a few other classmates would hit the court during recess and were adamant about referring to our clique as the WNBA. We were pretty decent, so I thought. Nonetheless, I'm sure Coco's dad is elated she followed her heart and was inspired at such a young age. Can you imagine what Coco's life would look like if she never saw Serena? Moreover, can you imagine if the Williams sisters didn't have the courage to keep showing up to play, surrounded by upper-class white families at these country clubs? They could've easily been intimidated being around players with different economic backgrounds or just because of their skin color. This trailblazing duo will continue to have an impact on black athletes all over, both women and men, for generations to come. This is their legacy.

So, as this chapter comes to a close, I want to leave you with this: people may box you in according to what they believe you were made for and your current ability. They may mean well, but they don't know who you are becoming. Don't allow them to deter you from following your heart and going after your dreams. You could be the reason someone has the courage to go after theirs. Regardless of what your current economic situation may tell you, where you live, or your skin color, if you believe in it, do it for you, Sis. Do all that you can do to make it happen, and don't stop until you reach your wildest dreams. It takes heart, courage, fortitude, and discipline. Always remember your gift is not just for you; it's for you to share with whoever is connected to your destiny. It takes a host and connection to create influence. You are the influencer someone needs to see.

The Entertainment Times
Deadlines

These come up all the time. You will always have deliverables to be met by a certain time; they are perhaps one of the best ways to stay organized. They keep you from procrastinating. I'd say, "They keep you on yo' toes!"

Timelines

Be mindful when promising a specific time for the completion of a task: especially when it is creative-based. You can mention time ranges but that may still bite you in the a$$. It is called overpromising and underdelivering. If this is a repeated offense, it then becomes the recipe for your team to start losing respect and trust in whether you can execute the job. It also ultimately puts your job in jeopardy.

I'm a creative at heart. We need time to get into a zone to create or sometimes that zone will present itself organically. I realized one of my weaknesses was organizational management, as I've mentioned. This consists of organizing, leading, controlling, and planning. Make plans?? What are *thozzzze*? I would just keep things in my head. Of course, that wasn't going to fly in this leadership role long-term, so I started working on setting small, realistic goals for myself in these areas, then for the team.

My question to you is: as a leader, what would you want to see your team accomplish? These can be daily, weekly, monthly, quarterly goals. The clearer you are about the vision for the team members, the better and sooner you can communicate it to them. That's true with anything in life. "Having strategies and systems in place will help you and the team work more efficiently." This just brings things back full-circle regarding the impact of your habits.

Use Your Time Wisely

Using time wisely doesn't only pertain to not wasting time, but also the timing in which you do things. It's hard enough to have to figure out what you need to say and the appropriate tone it should be delivered in. The next part of equation is whether now is a good time for you to share. We talked about maybe not having time to wait for a GOOD TIME to say something, but different from that is a Wise Time, which will always be a good time because it's influenced by that good ole intuition.

Let's say I'm in my MD role. We're about to hit the stage, and I just saw on a production email that a previously confirmed awards show has been cancelled. It's probably not a great time to tell the artist right before or even right after the show.

Also, know where you stand in rank if there are several leaders present. Obviously, you have to be cognizant of all official positions and understand their primary functions to not overstep. We covered a few of these previously, but in the music entertainment world, there's usually a hierarchy of leaders for an artist. From the top, you generally start with the A&R (Artist & Repertoire) rep, artist manager, production manager, tour manager, stage manager, then MD. This may vary depending on your discipline of entertainment, but is fairly standard in the music industry. Being informed does not obligate me to discuss the matter in the scenario presented. The manager generally works closest to the artist. It is their job to protect, communicate directly with, and make decisions that best suit the client. The manager is also the one to disperse such information. Now, at any point the artist may come to me regarding the calendar update; then we can talk. You want things to be done with decency and in order.

Here's another scenario featuring a music director:

So, we've been in 11-hour rehearsals all week preparing for tour. The artist usually comes in a few hours after the band. This gives everyone time to get settled so when the artist walks in, it's straight to the microphone. Time is always of the essence for them.

Now early in the day, a production email goes out, saying:

FOR THE LADIES

"Hey Team, our Saturday setlist needs to be only 45 minutes. We'll need to figure out what song to cut from the 50-minute set."

My MD thoughts on these threads WHILE ACTIVELY reading go a little like.... *Okay, is this venue indoors or outdoors? What city are we going to be in? What is the occasion? Make sure we don't cut a song that is relevant to the event. Do we have to cut an entire song? What songs have two verses? Are there wardrobe changes?*

Most likely at this point, the manager has already brought it to the artist's attention, but it would be best to be proactive and make direct contact if you have that relationship.

I was fortunate to have that experience with a few artists. The artist and MD should have the tightest bond and chemistry on stage. That starts from creating a strong one off-stage. The tale goes, you should never be friends with the artist. Hell, you better find a genuine way!

There are certainly some valid points as to why that adage exists. Famous people have a lot to protect and upkeep. It is a big risk to them and their band if the wrong person gets hold of some sensitive information. Even after signing an NDA, some people just lose control. Of course, I do understand the importance of protecting your privacy through boundaries; however, I believe we should place an emphasis more on the intention and expectation.

Intention: why do you really want to befriend the artist? Is it for clout, or to genuinely build so the creative collaboration process moves smoothly because you've spent Wise Time together?

Expectation: are you going to be asking them for money because work is slow or calling them on their cell all the time?

It's okay to be friends with the artist if you trust them, the energy feels real, and you know when to turn it on and off. Just be mindful that you don't get too comfortable in public and that you maintain respect for each role. I would encourage that dynamic.

It's Going to Take Time

Grace, consistency, and patience will be essential. Grace, when you feel the need to be too hard on yourself; patience, when you're frustrated and having a hard time with stumbling blocks and consistency, helping to get into the groove of things more efficiently. Leading in the entertainment industry is about finding the right rhythm. The more you dance to a song, the more fluid you become in your movement. You have a better sense of timing and can anticipate what's next because the song has been on replay. It's going to take time. There are many things to learn as is, but things will forever be changing. This business is constantly evolving with a heavy emphasis on what's trending in pop culture. With time, you will become wiser. With time, you will become more trusting. With time, you will become a more confident leader. With time, you will have more success stories to use as a teaching tool for your team.

Tour Tales with Tracyan
The Road to MD'ing Industry Artists

While there's a heavy emphasis placed on my experience as a music director in the industry, my real introduction to this job was becoming drum major in high school.

Being in the band in the South is a whole cultural experience. In addition, becoming a drum major is like going to boot camp: it will break you down before it builds you up. It was 70% mental and 30% physical. This may have been the most pivotal season for me in high school developing discipline in time management as I was also preparing for adulthood. I'm forever indebted to this experience that prepared me for the real world. Along the way post-drum major status, I started acquiring MD positions with local gospel groups in Atlanta, later expanding to Top 40s bands. Each stage offered more scenarios for me to build my skill set creatively and increase my business acumen. It was over a span of 11 years of practice between 2004 and 2015 before my first official industry call as Music Director with Melanie Fiona. Let's just say it took time.

So now it was 2018, just eight months into my tenure as a band member with Janelle Monáe, I was offered an official position as MD. There is no set time for such a promotion, however it is quite uncommon to be the 'quote on quote' new person and become the leader over the old heads with years in the game. I was the anomaly. The first gig out the gate was a tribute for Stevie Wonder, who was in attendance, among many other living legends. Had this been my first rodeo, I would easily have flubbed this day. First of all, fun fact, Stevie Wonder is my idol, and there we were getting ready to be a part of honoring him. My second thought was, *My first time in my new role is really about to be this epic! Yes, it is.* I was nervous all over again, to say the least, even with all the years of experience leading up to this moment.

We were still trying to sort out the setlist during sound check just hours before the show, but I didn't crack under pressure. You have to remain in character: as the memes say, KEEP CALM. No time to fold. We ended up having a great show and got to take pictures with Stevie. This was a historic night I'll never forget. Barely a month later, my second gig turned out to be the 61st GRAMMY Awards. I felt like I couldn't catch my breath but in the most amazing way. There's a scripture in the Bible that talks about God pouring out blessings so abundantly that you don't have enough room to receive them. That's what life was like. It seemed like the time was flying by and the caliber of gigs was becoming grander and grander. What had occurred to me was that I stood the test of time – from the time I was named drum major to landing one of the biggest MD roles of my career – because I stayed in the race.

The End

You may not always be able to keep track of time, but you always know when you've used it wisely. It will certainly show up in your performance and ability to deliver the task in the moment. Nothing incredibly great comes fast. Investments are a big lesson in delayed gratification. Being a leader can be a thankless job for a long time, but the thank-you will eventually come. Most importantly, the thank-you to self for understanding the value of time and using it wisely will be the biggest reward on your entertainment timeline. Time is truly one of the most valuable blessings we have and cannot get back.

Appointed vs Assigned Leader
When Purpose Takes the Wheel...

So, let's quickly look at the difference between being appointed and being assigned. Generally, the appointed person has a specific role or title. They most likely have school credits, certifications, degrees, or high levels of experience in their area of expertise. The assignment usually has everything to do with the task at hand, and that's where the assigned leader comes into play.

As an assigned leader, you don't need credentials from school. You don't need a letter of reference from an esteemed individual. You don't need a pat on the back. You can't ask for the assignment; it is a God-given gift. Consider this to be your calling and purpose in life, which you firmly believe and stand on. You understand this will be the piece/peace that makes up the difference in your shortcomings wherever you go. It's like the FLASH Pass to the Six Flags line that gets you to jump to the front without waiting. It's the approval over the underwriter's declined application. Ultimately, it's what gets you ahead when you are seemingly behind. It's the one divine thing that you can depend on when all else is against you. If we were in church right now, I'd be on the Hammond B3 organ backing up the pastor as they get happy preaching about the goodness of the assignment and how it makes the difference.

In entertainment leadership, sometimes there may be someone less qualified on paper but more qualified according to purpose. Purpose will always win over Paper in my book! It's the "WHY", the source of our mere existence. More importantly, let's also acknowledge that you can be appointed and assigned all in one. Now that's a special place to be!

Let's explore your life for a second. We're going to dig a little deeper into your relationship with a higher power here. Have you ever been in a position in which you're not the appointed leader, but you knew this was your Godly assignment? This is an area to which you've been called and where you feel comfortable because you're well versed with experience and have spiritual insight. How does one finagle their way into a public situation with their uninvited opinions and suggestions? This can certainly get tricky when trying to maneuver with a purposeful gift over the appointed leader. A key to getting around this is one simple word: *humility*. Someone once shared a quote with me: "Humility isn't thinking less of yourself, but thinking of yourself less." This isn't the time to think about what others will think of you. You can expect others to have thoughts of, "Oh, she thinks she's better than us. She just got here. She's trying to present herself in a way that the higher-ups will notice and promote her." Listen, if what you have to offer can benefit the whole team, you have to be courageous enough to step out on your own, regardless of everyone else's insecurities. 'Cause let's be honest, that's really the juice behind the haters. Don't be a gatekeeper, *Leading Industry Ladies*.

This is easier said than done for some of our passive counterparts who may naturally just let it cruise by. Don't play the role of the Pleasing Leader to try and keep the peace. Do not allow a title or lack thereof to keep you from assisting. This is your opportunity to live with purpose.

There are many things to keep in mind when finagling your way to jump into a public situation with a suggestion or opinion when you don't have a title. Consider this a friendly reminder that one of the most important things you can do is lead with humility. As it pertains to your delivery, you must be in tune with the timing and your team members' or colleague's demeanor. It's a delicate dance, especially when you are essentially correcting your peers, moreover, an adult man. I did not get to where I am by being passive, sweet, shy, and quiet all the time. It's perfectly normal to feel like you might rock the boat. PS, you're going to at some point, so go ahead and be assertive while you're at it.

There are a few strategies I have for addressing this:

As mentioned earlier, it's good to consider your co-worker's position and the best way to communicate with them. It may not be the best, most fun idea to correct individuals publicly, especially amongst other employees, so if you're comfortable, a simple side private convo with whomever needs correcting could resolve this. Having a trusted relationship is a plus when going straight to the source, which is something I've done before. Another way is to take it up with a higher ranked leader who could advise if you don't feel comfortable or safe.

Tour Tales with Tracyan Fantasia

The year was 2019, and I'd just secured my new gig with Fantasia in October. We were preparing for the Sketchbook Tour with Robin Thicke, Tank, and "Tasia" as the headliner. All the while, I was still juggling CeeLo and Janelle Monáe dates. "How?" is a great question! It sounds unreal and crazy in retrospect. Every artist required something different from me, be it serving as a multi-instrumentalist + background singer, or the duality of musician with music direction. This gig in particular, though, only called for me to play keyboards. I immediately assumed this hit would be a breeze. Interestingly enough, I didn't know this one would actually require more of my spiritual gift and insight.

There were so many new things happening. I was on a fresh healing journey from becoming sober and gaining a new outlook on life. I was reclaiming my time. Messing up and having faults will not necessarily impede upon your progress to operate in your gift. You can still be effective in ministry regardless of your circumstances. There was still a certain heaviness and shame that I silently carried but I was surrounded by so much love I had no choice but to start feeling better. For anyone who has survived the trenches and life's losses, you are that much more valuable to humanity because of your experiences. I was present and thankful every day that I got to do what I love for a living and live with purpose. I was gifted with music so people could be healed. It just made sense for me to be there with my powerful sister, Fantasia.

We had an MD — my idol Kim Burse again — and we had an onstage MD; this was delegation at its finest. Workload-wise, this was my least cumbersome tour physically, with only one discipline. Aside from keyboards, I was able to contribute to the creative arrangements and give input when Kim asked us to pitch some musical ideas in rehearsal.

For those of you who truly know Fantasia, you know she grew up in the church with southern roots. It's just in her wherever she goes. She puts on a show and brings the soul you never knew you needed. One thing we have in common is that we are both PKs – Pastor's Kids. We also have a good understanding of the importance of being in tune spiritually.

I have been a church musician over half my life, which has truly helped me to gain an understanding of the primary function of my role. It is our responsibility to help create an atmosphere conducive for praise and worship to go forth. We must understand our assignment is to be able to set the tone musically and shift in real time with finesse. Another part of our job is to underscore throughout the service — during the prayer, during the church announcements, while the preacher talks — and flow with them or the worship leader. Some things cannot be taught. You just have to grow up and be in it.

With that in mind, for the Sketchbook Tour, Fantasia had a gospel segment built into her set, rightfully so. She was very intentional about performing with purpose. Usually, the MD will utilize tracks to help guide and support the show for bigger venues; however, this gospel moment was all live. Remember, I was the keyboardist, so I had to carry quite a bit during the live church moments. No two shows were ever the same, even doing the same songs. That's how church goes. Our gospel medley included "Stand" by Donnie McClurkin, "Necessary" by Dennis Reed and GAP, and then we finished off with the "Ahhhhmens" from "Total Praise" by Richard Smallwood. The next song we transitioned into was "Baby Mama"!

What we noticed was people were still trying to recover from the mini church service during "Baby Mama." This song is an R&B anthem for single mothers. Though the message is positive and brings light to these hero women for their courage and strength, worshipping and praising God during "Baby Mama" was not the ideal vibe we were going for. Obviously, something needed to change but it wasn't immediately clear what revisions were needed in the setlist.

I got back in my church musician bag and started thinking about flow and finesse and what song would allow us to gracefully come out of that big moment. It hit me that "Lose to Win" provides a better emotional segue out of "Total Praise". Then we could get into the "Baby Mama" anthem. I wasn't her MD, but I took my idea directly to her. I was still working as Janelle's MD at the time, so building setlists was something fresh on my radar and I felt good about it.

At this point, Kim, who had been the head MD, had already fulfilled her duties and moved on to her next project. She left our onstage MD in charge to call the shots. Now, I admit, I did overstep my boundary in this moment by going straight to Tasia with my suggestion. Technically, I should have run it by our onstage MD first; however, I did apologize. I understand respecting chain

APPOINTED VS ASSIGNED LEADER

of commands, but also, T and I had established a great, solid, and trustworthy business/friendship in just the few weeks since we were introduced, which is why I felt comfortable going to her in the first place. We were tapped in early on. I'm sure a lot of it had to do with our upbringing in church and her just being cool and relatable. She immediately agreed with my thought and asked if we could change the show that night. I had already run it by our playback engineer, who mentioned it would be an easy switch just in case she wanted to pull the trigger. Ask me if I was prepared or not! LOL! I was in full-on "MD mode" even though I wasn't appointed. I just understood the assignment and what Fantasia wanted to happen both musically and internally. From that day on, we played the show with the updated setlist until the final tour date, and I couldn't have been prouder to play a small piece in the creative development of the 2019 Sketchbook Tour. I'll remember this for the rest of my life.

The End

Regardless of what genre of music I've associated myself with, I'll always have church in my blood. I like to say the anointing cancels protocol. Basically, you can be underqualified, not appointed, the newest member on the team, but when God blesses you with a gift, you end up gaining entry to places that you normally wouldn't have access to. Consider it a portal of favor and grace to your supernatural power. This is the global entry that will allow your purpose to take the wheel. I didn't wait for someone to ask if I had a suggestion because I was intuitive and sure about what I knew would work. You have to get to that point in your life where you don't care what anyone thinks of you. I didn't allow someone's opinion or title to keep me from being informed of my impact in the camp. There are talented people and then there are gifted people. Your gift holds something special that school or life can't give you. It comes from God and has a purpose to change how someone feels or enhance how they experience life. When you are humble and confident in knowing how people can benefit from your gift, you're less likely to doubt yourself. You have the opportunity to help change someone's life or career and understand that you don't need a title to confirm who you are. It is at this point that you'll be able to complete the assignment.

Feminine vs Masculine Energy

As much as we like to associate femininity and masculinity with gender, they are not limited to one or the other; both men and women share the same traits. I truly believe it was God's gift to help us better comprehend why we make the decisions we make. I see it as an unspoken form of communication and understanding.

While mothers are thought to be more nurturing, fathers are just as capable as it pertains to children. Perhaps their methods aren't always exactly the same; however, the translation still shows up with the intention of love no matter what age. Even if it's tough love, the common denominator is the giver ultimately just wants the best for you. Therefore, being able to nurture can work with anyone, parent or not. It has been said men are providers/givers and women are receivers, but consider that each gender does both. I believe giving can be a masculine and feminine trait however receiving appeals more to the feminine side. That is my personal opinion. A

FOR THE LADIES

leader is a professional giver by trade, whether you realize it or not. You constantly give and provide by any means necessary. Followers are natural receivers. What good is it to follow something that doesn't offer a viable output?

To be a great leader, you must be a dynamic follower. This is a telltale sign you're able to move in your feminine power. Generally speaking, when you hear "assertive", you may associate it with making power moves; however, moving with grace is also a power move. Moving with grace is a beautiful act of self-control and humility. As mentioned before, humility is not thinking less of yourself but thinking of yourself less. The level of humility in which you operate will always show up outwardly. Here is where you are considerate, caring, patient, mindful, in-tune, insightful, open-minded, passionate, thoughtful, and willing to let someone else go before you. While women may typically have these down pat, it may take some of us longer to tap into it. Then you have some men who ace all of these with flying colors thus proving these feminine traits are not limited to gender roles.

I used to be self-conscious, feeling like I wasn't "feminine" or pretty enough. As a child, I was a tomboy—wasn't really into "girly things" such as baby dolls, makeup, and purses; I hung out with the guys and quite frankly just felt more comfortable around them. I just wasn't like my female classmates. I was a jeans-every-day, T-shirt, ponytail-wearing kind of girl. I wasn't interested in dressing cute or whateva'. I just wanted to be comfy.

Now, as a leader your visual representation is just as essential as your audible delivery. We live in a world where so many women are being over-sexualized and

FEMININE VS MASCULINE ENERGY

criticized yet somehow still glorified. You can be as assertive as you would like to, but if you got hips and dips doing tricks on these guys' eyes, good luck! Not all, but some of them are going to listen with their eyes, women included. This also goes for looking dusty. Showing up to work looking any old kind of way matters too. In the entertainment industry, there are a lot of eccentric people. We can get away with quite a few eclectic things when it comes to attire. The rules are a little looser than a corporate job's dress code. Just ask yourself, is this 'fit' appropriate for my job as a leader today?

I can remember my mom telling me in my preteens, "You need to start wearing a purse because that's what young ladies do." I obliged, but all I had in there was some Chapstick—not even lip gloss. Nailed it. I mistook femininity for being girly. There goes that gender role association again. It wasn't until my 30s that I finally embraced the realization that I'd been feminine enough all along. I'd checked off the list of humility two times over. I was considerate, was sensitive to my surroundings and colleagues, was caring, and had the ability to nurture when necessary, amongst many other attributes. To be a dynamic leader, we must be intuitive and learn to trust our gut.

> *"I strongly believe one of the greatest gifts God gave us was our intuition."*

I've taken a moment to identify what some of my traits are on both spectrums. After you read mine, consider jotting down yours.

Feminine Side: Reads energy well, very intuitive, patient, care-full, understanding & empathetic.

FOR THE LADIES

Masculine Side: Very matter-of-fact and bottom line, straight shooter, not as patient, more of a risk-taker, logic over emotion.

You have to be in common spaces with guys outside of your work environment just as much as you need to be around women. This will help you become more comfortable speaking to men and understanding a little more of how they think. To my advantage, I was naturally a tomboy, so there were no issues being around the guys. Before I even considered being a musician, I was outside playing basketball and football with the neighbor's sons. It's crazy how your childhood influences and impacts your adulthood. My Christmas gifts were even "for boys", hence the remote-controlled monster truck. I'll never forget that. Thanks, Mommy Bug and Dad. If anything, I felt less comfortable hanging with the girls. You were not about to catch me playing with baby dolls and fake makeup. Needless to say, I had some catching up to do with the ladies so I wouldn't be socially awkward.

Women feed off each other's feminism. Ladies, when we get that dramatic…Guuurrrrrrrrrrrrrrrrrrrr! Step 1. You already know WE FINNA GET ALL THE TEA and good DEETS, cause that's what we do with our said friends and family. Now let's park this truck here… Skurrrrttt. In a professional setting, when talking to men — not all, but SOME of them… okay MOST of them — are not interested in hearing a full explanation and all the details. Let's be honest. Businesswomen also don't care for the long-drawn-out answer. This may be okay if your colleague is truly like a sister or homegirl to you, but you have to remember when to turn on the profesh side. Let's look at these scenarios below with the consideration that this could be a female or male you're responding to.

FEMININE VS MASCULINE ENERGY

Scenario 1

Manager: Hey, Tiffany, did you confirm the guest mic with production?

Answer #1

Tiffany: So, I had pulled up to the venue, then saw so and so's camp and chopped it up with them thennnnn realized our homeboi James was on the hit too so it was lowkey a reunion, but I told them I was running to complete something. They haven't confirmed yet.

Answer #2

Tiffany: I did check and not yet, but I'll circle back.

When speaking to a professional, be it a man or a woman, ask yourself, "What is it that they absolutely NEED to know in this moment?" Once you figure that out and get rid of the fluff (unnecessary additional information), dive right in and be done. This may mean adjusting a few words depending on your audience if your intended delivery of the message is too direct. It should be palatable for the receiver.

Now, there are cases in full company settings where you'll need to say more, even if it doesn't pertain to a certain entity. This is good in a sense for a better understanding of all the working and moving parts it takes to steer the ship. This also brings awareness to the importance and impact of how your performance affects the next person's. I may not be able to do the dance, but I understand if I don't deliver the music in time, it's going to greatly affect the dancers' process of creating choreography within the timeline.

FOR THE LADIES

Scenario 2

Secretary: Hey, Leslie, do you know when the audit is?

Answer #1

Leslie: I don't know.

Answer #2

Leslie: I don't know at this moment, but let me make a call and see if we can verify that.

Here's a case in which saying more... is saying more. When being thorough matters. Saying, "I don't know" when you haven't exhausted every option to find the answer is greatly frowned upon. Your best bet is to rely on sheer professionalism by being proactive and making calls to handle it. It is a good thing and always will be. At some point, the two energies will crossbreed and create a beautiful harmony that allows you to lead with confidence and grace. Rest assured, with time, you will get better and better — day by day, step by step, and minute by minute — as long as you stay in the race. The game is still going on even when there is a time-out, but the moment you quit, that's it. Stay focused on your why. That's the finish line. Finishing is important; moreover, how you finish is critical because it's the first and last thing you'll remember and be remembered by.

Ladies, how are we doing? Are we feeling positive about all we've discussed?

Becoming an Entertainment Leader

If you are to become the leader God intended you to be, it starts and ends with how you lead and carry yourself. The word "become" has everything to do with transforming, growing, and changing. Every opportunity in this industry that you have to learn and apply contributes to the evolution of your development, good and bad. Where there are no life-altering events, there's no space for a shift and growth to take place. What I'm saying is, we all need curve balls thrown at us to build our strength, patience, and character. Throughout this book, we've navigated through different scenarios, circumstances, economic statuses, and the environments that influence and affect our day-to-day decision-making. When you're afraid, lonely, and doubting yourself, and stress kicks in, remember you're serving a purpose for the greater good. As mentioned before, you won't always have the answers and that's okay. This territory of leadership will continue to require you to explore and take risks when you're not sure and depend on your counterparts. Even when you know exactly what you're doing, you're still taking a chance.

One day you may feel like you're on top of the world and then the next you may question a higher power, asking "Why me?" Instead of "Why me, God?" how about humbly asking "Why not me?" You've spent years being prepared and procured for this season of your life. Those challenges with becoming who you're meant to be pale in comparison to the reward God has for you. There will always be people who are more qualified on paper and experience based on tenure; however, those who are called and chosen by a divine being are still likely to do just as well simply because they are assigned and anointed for the task.

When life becomes overwhelming, make sure you have an outlet for social rest. It is simply taking a break from your stressors by surrounding yourself with positive, affirming people or activities that lift your spirits. Therapy is a great source to consider if you haven't done so. Things don't have to be bad for there to be a need for a therapist. Major life changes just may be hard to process, so a cushion to help is a beautiful gift you can give yourself. Tap into your hobbies and take a step away when necessary. Some of mine are hiking, listening to motivational podcasts, watching a comedy, bowling, playing with my dog, having a girls' day at brunch, or going to hear live music. Music has the power to calm a savage beast, so it can certainly help you manage and regulate anxiety and emotions. Your mental, spiritual, and physical health will improve with time. I truly believe you'll experience the benefits of being kind to yourself when you take a moment to reset. You are the frontline soldier and have to be conditioned for the battle and marathon ahead to become what you're on earth for. May your weapons be power, patience, and perseverance. I pray that your life will be enriched, protected, and covered by your courage to make decisions for the betterment of you and the team. Walk with wisdom, speak with authority, and move with excellence, my beautiful sister. Thank you for reading my first book and investing in you.

Warm regards,
Tracyan

I wish you all the best....

About the Author

Tracyan Martin, an Atlanta native, is the creator of "Pop & Piano", a professional multi-instrumentalist, an endorsed artist, and a rising author. Her touring career launched in 2009 with Musiq Soulchild, and since then, she has held prominent roles such as the Regional Chapter Lead for Jammcard Atlanta and Music Director for artists like Melanie Fiona, Janelle Monáe, and CeeLo. Tracyan has collaborated with a wide array of talents, including Melanie Martinez, Fantasia, and Darwin Hobbs. Her live performances and featured credits span prestigious platforms like The 61st GRAMMY Awards, *Good Morning America*, *The Voice*, and *The Urban One Honors*.

Tracyan has completed several national and international tours, including Oprah's 2020 Vision Tour, where she showcased her skills on both keytar and trombone. Her debut single, "Lifetime of Love", featuring her on vocals, Wurlitzer, and trombone, soared into the top 20 on the UK Breaking Artists charts. Currently, she is captivating audiences on the Las Vegas Strip, performing with Cirque Du Soleil's newest show, MAD APPLE, at the New York-New York Hotel and Casino.

Renowned for her "can-do" attitude and commitment to excellence, Tracyan has earned acclaim as a trusted industry professional. Her mission is to continue inspiring leading industry ladies, and reach new heights in her own career.

My Notes

MY NOTES

FOR THE LADIES

MY NOTES

FOR THE LADIES

MY NOTES

FOR THE LADIES

MY NOTES

FOR THE LADIES

MY NOTES

FOR THE LADIES

MY NOTES

FOR THE LADIES

MY NOTES

FOR THE LADIES

MY NOTES

FOR THE LADIES

MY NOTES

FOR THE LADIES

MY NOTES

FOR THE LADIES

MY NOTES

FOR THE LADIES

MY NOTES

FOR THE LADIES

MY NOTES

FOR THE LADIES

Made in the USA
Columbia, SC
23 April 2025